Caregiver daily
Log Book

Personal Information

Name	
Phone	
Address	

Caregiving Notes for						Date		
Toileting	Time							
	U							
	BM							
Waking Up at Night								
Breakfast								
AM Snack								
Lunch								
PM Snack								
Dinner								
Drinks								

Activities

Appointments

Health Concerns

Plans for Tommorow

Pain Level

Happiness Level

Alertness Level

Supplies Needed Soon

Medication Taken

Notes

Caregiving Notes for							Date		
Toileting	Time								
	U								
	BM								
Waking Up at Night									
Breakfast									
AM Snack									
Lunch									
PM Snack									
Dinner									
Drinks									

Activities	

Appointments	
Health Concerns	
Plans for Tommorow	
Pain Level	
Happiness Level	
Alertness Level	
Supplies Needed Soon	
Medication Taken	

Notes	

Caregiving Notes for						Date		
Toileting	Time							
	U							
	BM							
Waking Up at Night								
Breakfast								
AM Snack								
Lunch								
PM Snack								
Dinner								
Drinks								

Activities

Appointments	
Health Concerns	
Plans for Tommorow	
Pain Level	
Happiness Level	
Alertness Level	
Supplies Needed Soon	
Medication Taken	

Notes

Caregiving Notes for						Date		
Toileting Time								
U								
BM								
Waking Up at Night								
Breakfast								
AM Snack								
Lunch								
PM Snack								
Dinner								
Drinks								

Activities

Appointments	
Health Concerns	
Plans for Tommorow	
Pain Level	
Happiness Level	
Alertness Level	
Supplies Needed Soon	
Medication Taken	

Notes

Caregiving Notes for						Date		
Toileting	Time							
	U							
	BM							
Waking Up at Night								
Breakfast								
AM Snack								
Lunch								
PM Snack								
Dinner								
Drinks								

Activities

Appointments

Health Concerns

Plans for Tommorow

Pain Level

Happiness Level

Alertness Level

Supplies Needed Soon

Medication Taken

Notes

Caregiving Notes for						Date		
Toileting	Time							
	U							
	BM							
Waking Up at Night								
Breakfast								
AM Snack								
Lunch								
PM Snack								
Dinner								
Drinks								

Activities	

Appointments	
Health Concerns	
Plans for Tommorow	
Pain Level	
Happiness Level	
Alertness Level	
Supplies Needed Soon	
Medication Taken	

Notes	

Caregiving Notes for						Date		
Toileting	Time							
	U							
	BM							
Waking Up at Night								

Breakfast	
AM Snack	
Lunch	
PM Snack	
Dinner	
Drinks	

Activities	

Appointments	
Health Concerns	
Plans for Tommorow	
Pain Level	
Happiness Level	
Alertness Level	
Supplies Needed Soon	
Medication Taken	

Notes	

Caregiving Notes for						Date		

Toileting	Time							
	U							
	BM							

Waking Up at Night			

Breakfast	
AM Snack	
Lunch	
PM Snack	
Dinner	
Drinks	

Activities	

Appointments	
Health Concerns	
Plans for Tommorow	
Pain Level	
Happiness Level	
Alertness Level	
Supplies Needed Soon	
Medication Taken	

Notes	

Caregiving Notes for						Date		
Toileting	Time							
	U							
	BM							
Waking Up at Night								
Breakfast								
AM Snack								
Lunch								
PM Snack								
Dinner								
Drinks								

Activities	

Appointments	
Health Concerns	
Plans for Tommorow	
Pain Level	
Happiness Level	
Alertness Level	
Supplies Needed Soon	
Medication Taken	

Notes	

Caregiving Notes for						Date		
Toileting	Time							
	U							
	BM							
Waking Up at Night								
Breakfast								
AM Snack								
Lunch								
PM Snack								
Dinner								
Drinks								

Activities	

Appointments	
Health Concerns	
Plans for Tommorow	
Pain Level	
Happiness Level	
Alertness Level	
Supplies Needed Soon	
Medication Taken	

Notes	

Caregiving Notes for						Date		
Toileting	Time							
	U							
	BM							
Waking Up at Night								
Breakfast								
AM Snack								
Lunch								
PM Snack								
Dinner								
Drinks								

Activities

Appointments	
Health Concerns	
Plans for Tommorow	
Pain Level	
Happiness Level	
Alertness Level	
Supplies Needed Soon	
Medication Taken	

Notes

Caregiving Notes for						Date			
Toileting	Time								
	U								
	BM								
Waking Up at Night									
Breakfast									
AM Snack									
Lunch									
PM Snack									
Dinner									
Drinks									

Activities	

Appointments	
Health Concerns	
Plans for Tommorow	
Pain Level	
Happiness Level	
Alertness Level	
Supplies Needed Soon	
Medication Taken	

Notes	

Caregiving Notes for						Date		

Toileting	Time							
	U							
	BM							

Waking Up at Night			

Breakfast	
AM Snack	
Lunch	
PM Snack	
Dinner	
Drinks	

Activities	

Appointments	
Health Concerns	
Plans for Tommorow	
Pain Level	
Happiness Level	
Alertness Level	
Supplies Needed Soon	
Medication Taken	

Notes	

Caregiving Notes for						Date		
Toileting	Time							
	U							
	BM							
Waking Up at Night								
Breakfast								
AM Snack								
Lunch								
PM Snack								
Dinner								
Drinks								

Activities	

Appointments	
Health Concerns	
Plans for Tommorow	
Pain Level	
Happiness Level	
Alertness Level	
Supplies Needed Soon	
Medication Taken	

Notes	

Caregiving Notes for						Date		
Toileting	Time							
	U							
	BM							
Waking Up at Night								

Breakfast	
AM Snack	
Lunch	
PM Snack	
Dinner	
Drinks	

Activities	

Appointments	
Health Concerns	
Plans for Tommorow	
Pain Level	
Happiness Level	
Alertness Level	
Supplies Needed Soon	
Medication Taken	

Notes	

Caregiving Notes for						Date		
Toileting	Time							
	U							
	BM							
Waking Up at Night								
Breakfast								
AM Snack								
Lunch								
PM Snack								
Dinner								
Drinks								

Activities	

Appointments	
Health Concerns	
Plans for Tommorow	
Pain Level	
Happiness Level	
Alertness Level	
Supplies Needed Soon	
Medication Taken	

Notes	

Caregiving Notes for						Date		
Toileting	Time							
	U							
	BM							
Waking Up at Night								

Breakfast	
AM Snack	
Lunch	
PM Snack	
Dinner	
Drinks	

Activities	

Appointments	
Health Concerns	
Plans for Tommorow	
Pain Level	
Happiness Level	
Alertness Level	
Supplies Needed Soon	
Medication Taken	

Notes	

Caregiving Notes for						Date			
Toileting	Time								
	U								
	BM								
Waking Up at Night									

Breakfast	
AM Snack	
Lunch	
PM Snack	
Dinner	
Drinks	

Activities	

Appointments	
Health Concerns	
Plans for Tommorow	
Pain Level	
Happiness Level	
Alertness Level	
Supplies Needed Soon	
Medication Taken	

Notes	

Caregiving Notes for							Date		
Toileting	Time								
	U								
	BM								
Waking Up at Night									

Breakfast	
AM Snack	
Lunch	
PM Snack	
Dinner	
Drinks	

Activities	

Appointments	
Health Concerns	
Plans for Tommorow	
Pain Level	
Happiness Level	
Alertness Level	
Supplies Needed Soon	
Medication Taken	

Notes	

Caregiving Notes for						Date		
Toileting	Time							
	U							
	BM							
Waking Up at Night								
Breakfast								
AM Snack								
Lunch								
PM Snack								
Dinner								
Drinks								

Activities

Appointments	
Health Concerns	
Plans for Tommorow	
Pain Level	
Happiness Level	
Alertness Level	
Supplies Needed Soon	
Medication Taken	

Notes

Caregiving Notes for						Date		
Toileting	Time							
	U							
	BM							
Waking Up at Night								

Breakfast	
AM Snack	
Lunch	
PM Snack	
Dinner	
Drinks	

Activities	

Appointments	
Health Concerns	
Plans for Tommorow	
Pain Level	
Happiness Level	
Alertness Level	
Supplies Needed Soon	
Medication Taken	

Notes	

Caregiving Notes for						Date		
Toileting	Time							
	U							
	BM							
Waking Up at Night								
Breakfast								
AM Snack								
Lunch								
PM Snack								
Dinner								
Drinks								

Activities

Appointments	
Health Concerns	
Plans for Tommorow	
Pain Level	
Happiness Level	
Alertness Level	
Supplies Needed Soon	
Medication Taken	

Notes

Caregiving Notes for						Date		
Toileting	Time							
	U							
	BM							
Waking Up at Night								
Breakfast								
AM Snack								
Lunch								
PM Snack								
Dinner								
Drinks								

Activities

Appointments	
Health Concerns	
Plans for Tommorow	
Pain Level	
Happiness Level	
Alertness Level	
Supplies Needed Soon	
Medication Taken	

Notes

Caregiving Notes for						Date		
Toileting	Time							
	U							
	BM							
Waking Up at Night								
Breakfast								
AM Snack								
Lunch								
PM Snack								
Dinner								
Drinks								

Activities

Appointments	
Health Concerns	
Plans for Tommorow	
Pain Level	
Happiness Level	
Alertness Level	
Supplies Needed Soon	
Medication Taken	

Notes

Caregiving Notes for						Date		
Toileting	Time							
	U							
	BM							
Waking Up at Night								
Breakfast								
AM Snack								
Lunch								
PM Snack								
Dinner								
Drinks								

Activities

Appointments	
Health Concerns	
Plans for Tommorow	
Pain Level	
Happiness Level	
Alertness Level	
Supplies Needed Soon	
Medication Taken	

Notes

Caregiving Notes for						Date		
Toileting	Time							
	U							
	BM							
Waking Up at Night								
Breakfast								
AM Snack								
Lunch								
PM Snack								
Dinner								
Drinks								

Activities	

Appointments	
Health Concerns	
Plans for Tommorow	
Pain Level	
Happiness Level	
Alertness Level	
Supplies Needed Soon	
Medication Taken	

Notes	

Caregiving Notes for						Date		
Toileting	Time							
	U							
	BM							
Waking Up at Night								
Breakfast								
AM Snack								
Lunch								
PM Snack								
Dinner								
Drinks								

Activities	

Appointments	
Health Concerns	
Plans for Tommorow	
Pain Level	
Happiness Level	
Alertness Level	
Supplies Needed Soon	
Medication Taken	

Notes	

Caregiving Notes for						Date		
Toileting	Time							
	U							
	BM							
Waking Up at Night								
Breakfast								
AM Snack								
Lunch								
PM Snack								
Dinner								
Drinks								

Activities	

Appointments	
Health Concerns	
Plans for Tommorow	
Pain Level	
Happiness Level	
Alertness Level	
Supplies Needed Soon	
Medication Taken	

Notes	

Caregiving Notes for						Date		
Toileting	Time							
	U							
	BM							
Waking Up at Night								
Breakfast								
AM Snack								
Lunch								
PM Snack								
Dinner								
Drinks								

Activities

Appointments	
Health Concerns	
Plans for Tommorow	
Pain Level	
Happiness Level	
Alertness Level	
Supplies Needed Soon	
Medication Taken	

Notes

Caregiving Notes for						Date		
Toileting	Time							
	U							
	BM							
Waking Up at Night								
Breakfast								
AM Snack								
Lunch								
PM Snack								
Dinner								
Drinks								
Activities								
Appointments								
Health Concerns								
Plans for Tommorow								
Pain Level								
Happiness Level								
Alertness Level								
Supplies Needed Soon								
Medication Taken								
Notes								

Caregiving Notes for						Date		
Toileting	Time							
	U							
	BM							
Waking Up at Night								
Breakfast								
AM Snack								
Lunch								
PM Snack								
Dinner								
Drinks								

Activities	

Appointments	
Health Concerns	
Plans for Tommorow	
Pain Level	
Happiness Level	
Alertness Level	
Supplies Needed Soon	
Medication Taken	

Notes	

Caregiving Notes for								
Date								

Toileting	Time							
	U							
	BM							

Waking Up at Night			

Breakfast	
AM Snack	
Lunch	
PM Snack	
Dinner	
Drinks	

Activities	

Appointments	
Health Concerns	
Plans for Tommorow	
Pain Level	
Happiness Level	
Alertness Level	
Supplies Needed Soon	
Medication Taken	

Notes	

Caregiving Notes for						Date		
Toileting	Time							
	U							
	BM							
Waking Up at Night								

Breakfast	
AM Snack	
Lunch	
PM Snack	
Dinner	
Drinks	

Activities	

Appointments	
Health Concerns	
Plans for Tommorow	
Pain Level	
Happiness Level	
Alertness Level	
Supplies Needed Soon	
Medication Taken	

Notes	

Caregiving Notes for						Date		
Toileting	Time							
	U							
	BM							
Waking Up at Night								
Breakfast								
AM Snack								
Lunch								
PM Snack								
Dinner								
Drinks								

Activities	

Appointments	
Health Concerns	
Plans for Tommorow	
Pain Level	
Happiness Level	
Alertness Level	
Supplies Needed Soon	
Medication Taken	

Notes	

Caregiving Notes for						Date		
Toileting	Time							
	U							
	BM							
Waking Up at Night								
Breakfast								
AM Snack								
Lunch								
PM Snack								
Dinner								
Drinks								

Activities	

Appointments	
Health Concerns	
Plans for Tommorow	
Pain Level	
Happiness Level	
Alertness Level	
Supplies Needed Soon	
Medication Taken	

Notes	

Caregiving Notes for									Date		
Toileting	Time										
	U										
	BM										
Waking Up at Night											
Breakfast											
AM Snack											
Lunch											
PM Snack											
Dinner											
Drinks											

Activities

Appointments	
Health Concerns	
Plans for Tommorow	
Pain Level	
Happiness Level	
Alertness Level	
Supplies Needed Soon	
Medication Taken	

Notes

Caregiving Notes for						Date		
Toileting	Time							
	U							
	BM							
Waking Up at Night								
Breakfast								
AM Snack								
Lunch								
PM Snack								
Dinner								
Drinks								

Activities

Appointments	
Health Concerns	
Plans for Tommorow	
Pain Level	
Happiness Level	
Alertness Level	
Supplies Needed Soon	
Medication Taken	

Notes

Caregiving Notes for						Date		
Toileting	Time							
	U							
	BM							
Waking Up at Night								
Breakfast								
AM Snack								
Lunch								
PM Snack								
Dinner								
Drinks								

Activities

Appointments	
Health Concerns	
Plans for Tommorow	
Pain Level	
Happiness Level	
Alertness Level	
Supplies Needed Soon	
Medication Taken	

Notes

Caregiving Notes for							Date		
Toileting	Time								
	U								
	BM								
Waking Up at Night									
Breakfast									
AM Snack									
Lunch									
PM Snack									
Dinner									
Drinks									

Activities	

Appointments	
Health Concerns	
Plans for Tommorow	
Pain Level	
Happiness Level	
Alertness Level	
Supplies Needed Soon	
Medication Taken	

Notes	

Caregiving Notes for						Date		
Toileting	Time							
	U							
	BM							
Waking Up at Night								
Breakfast								
AM Snack								
Lunch								
PM Snack								
Dinner								
Drinks								

Activities	

Appointments	
Health Concerns	
Plans for Tommorow	
Pain Level	
Happiness Level	
Alertness Level	
Supplies Needed Soon	
Medication Taken	

Notes	

Caregiving Notes for					Date		
Toileting Time							
U							
BM							
Waking Up at Night							

Breakfast	
AM Snack	
Lunch	
PM Snack	
Dinner	
Drinks	

Activities

Appointments	
Health Concerns	
Plans for Tommorow	
Pain Level	
Happiness Level	
Alertness Level	
Supplies Needed Soon	
Medication Taken	

Notes

Caregiving Notes for						Date		
Toileting	Time							
	U							
	BM							
Waking Up at Night								
Breakfast								
AM Snack								
Lunch								
PM Snack								
Dinner								
Drinks								

Activities

Appointments

Health Concerns

Plans for Tommorow

Pain Level

Happiness Level

Alertness Level

Supplies Needed Soon

Medication Taken

Notes

Caregiving Notes for						Date		
Toileting	Time							
	U							
	BM							
Waking Up at Night								
Breakfast								
AM Snack								
Lunch								
PM Snack								
Dinner								
Drinks								

Activities

Appointments	
Health Concerns	
Plans for Tommorow	
Pain Level	
Happiness Level	
Alertness Level	
Supplies Needed Soon	
Medication Taken	

Notes

Caregiving Notes for						Date		
Toileting	Time							
	U							
	BM							
Waking Up at Night								
Breakfast								
AM Snack								
Lunch								
PM Snack								
Dinner								
Drinks								

Activities

Appointments	
Health Concerns	
Plans for Tommorow	
Pain Level	
Happiness Level	
Alertness Level	
Supplies Needed Soon	
Medication Taken	

Notes

Caregiving Notes for						Date		
Toileting	Time							
	U							
	BM							
Waking Up at Night								
Breakfast								
AM Snack								
Lunch								
PM Snack								
Dinner								
Drinks								

Activities

Appointments	
Health Concerns	
Plans for Tommorow	
Pain Level	
Happiness Level	
Alertness Level	
Supplies Needed Soon	
Medication Taken	

Notes

Caregiving Notes for						Date		
Toileting	Time							
	U							
	BM							
Waking Up at Night								
Breakfast								
AM Snack								
Lunch								
PM Snack								
Dinner								
Drinks								

Activities

Appointments	
Health Concerns	
Plans for Tommorow	
Pain Level	
Happiness Level	
Alertness Level	
Supplies Needed Soon	
Medication Taken	

Notes

Caregiving Notes for						Date		
Toileting	Time							
	U							
	BM							
Waking Up at Night								
Breakfast								
AM Snack								
Lunch								
PM Snack								
Dinner								
Drinks								

Activities

Appointments	
Health Concerns	
Plans for Tommorow	
Pain Level	
Happiness Level	
Alertness Level	
Supplies Needed Soon	
Medication Taken	

Notes

Caregiving Notes for						Date		
Toileting	Time							
	U							
	BM							
Waking Up at Night								
Breakfast								
AM Snack								
Lunch								
PM Snack								
Dinner								
Drinks								

Activities

Appointments	
Health Concerns	
Plans for Tommorow	
Pain Level	
Happiness Level	
Alertness Level	
Supplies Needed Soon	
Medication Taken	

Notes

Caregiving Notes for						Date			
Toileting	Time								
	U								
	BM								
Waking Up at Night									
Breakfast									
AM Snack									
Lunch									
PM Snack									
Dinner									
Drinks									

Activities	

Appointments	
Health Concerns	
Plans for Tommorow	
Pain Level	
Happiness Level	
Alertness Level	
Supplies Needed Soon	
Medication Taken	

Notes	

Caregiving Notes for						Date			
Toileting	Time								
	U								
	BM								
Waking Up at Night									
Breakfast									
AM Snack									
Lunch									
PM Snack									
Dinner									
Drinks									

Activities

Appointments	
Health Concerns	
Plans for Tommorow	
Pain Level	
Happiness Level	
Alertness Level	
Supplies Needed Soon	
Medication Taken	

Notes

Caregiving Notes for						Date		
Toileting Time								
U								
BM								
Waking Up at Night								
Breakfast								
AM Snack								
Lunch								
PM Snack								
Dinner								
Drinks								

Activities

Appointments	
Health Concerns	
Plans for Tommorow	
Pain Level	
Happiness Level	
Alertness Level	
Supplies Needed Soon	
Medication Taken	

Notes

Caregiving Notes for						Date		
Toileting	Time							
	U							
	BM							
Waking Up at Night								
Breakfast								
AM Snack								
Lunch								
PM Snack								
Dinner								
Drinks								

Activities	

Appointments	
Health Concerns	
Plans for Tommorow	
Pain Level	
Happiness Level	
Alertness Level	
Supplies Needed Soon	
Medication Taken	

Notes	

Caregiving Notes for						Date		
Toileting	Time							
	U							
	BM							
Waking Up at Night								
Breakfast								
AM Snack								
Lunch								
PM Snack								
Dinner								
Drinks								

Activities	

Appointments	
Health Concerns	
Plans for Tommorow	
Pain Level	
Happiness Level	
Alertness Level	
Supplies Needed Soon	
Medication Taken	

Notes	

Caregiving Notes for						Date		
Toileting	Time							
	U							
	BM							
Waking Up at Night								
Breakfast								
AM Snack								
Lunch								
PM Snack								
Dinner								
Drinks								

Activities

Appointments	
Health Concerns	
Plans for Tommorow	
Pain Level	
Happiness Level	
Alertness Level	
Supplies Needed Soon	
Medication Taken	

Notes

Caregiving Notes for									Date		

	Time							
Toileting	U							
	BM							

Waking Up at Night		

Breakfast	
AM Snack	
Lunch	
PM Snack	
Dinner	
Drinks	

Activities	

Appointments	
Health Concerns	
Plans for Tommorow	
Pain Level	
Happiness Level	
Alertness Level	
Supplies Needed Soon	
Medication Taken	

Notes	

Caregiving Notes for						Date		
Toileting	Time							
	U							
	BM							
Waking Up at Night								
Breakfast								
AM Snack								
Lunch								
PM Snack								
Dinner								
Drinks								

Activities

Appointments	
Health Concerns	
Plans for Tommorow	
Pain Level	
Happiness Level	
Alertness Level	
Supplies Needed Soon	
Medication Taken	

Notes

Caregiving Notes for						Date		
Toileting	Time							
	U							
	BM							
Waking Up at Night								
Breakfast								
AM Snack								
Lunch								
PM Snack								
Dinner								
Drinks								

Activities	

Appointments	
Health Concerns	
Plans for Tommorow	
Pain Level	
Happiness Level	
Alertness Level	
Supplies Needed Soon	
Medication Taken	

Notes	

Caregiving Notes for						Date		
Toileting	Time							
	U							
	BM							
Waking Up at Night								
Breakfast								
AM Snack								
Lunch								
PM Snack								
Dinner								
Drinks								

Activities

Appointments	
Health Concerns	
Plans for Tommorow	
Pain Level	
Happiness Level	
Alertness Level	
Supplies Needed Soon	
Medication Taken	

Notes

Caregiving Notes for						Date		
Toileting Time								
U								
BM								
Waking Up at Night								
Breakfast								
AM Snack								
Lunch								
PM Snack								
Dinner								
Drinks								

Activities

Appointments	
Health Concerns	
Plans for Tommorow	
Pain Level	
Happiness Level	
Alertness Level	
Supplies Needed Soon	
Medication Taken	

Notes

Caregiving Notes for						Date		
Toileting	Time							
	U							
	BM							
Waking Up at Night								
Breakfast								
AM Snack								
Lunch								
PM Snack								
Dinner								
Drinks								

Activities

Appointments	
Health Concerns	
Plans for Tommorow	
Pain Level	
Happiness Level	
Alertness Level	
Supplies Needed Soon	
Medication Taken	

Notes

Caregiving Notes for						Date		
Toileting	Time							
	U							
	BM							
Waking Up at Night								
Breakfast								
AM Snack								
Lunch								
PM Snack								
Dinner								
Drinks								

Activities

Appointments	
Health Concerns	
Plans for Tommorow	
Pain Level	
Happiness Level	
Alertness Level	
Supplies Needed Soon	
Medication Taken	

Notes

Caregiving Notes for						Date		
Toileting	Time							
	U							
	BM							
Waking Up at Night								
Breakfast								
AM Snack								
Lunch								
PM Snack								
Dinner								
Drinks								

Activities

Appointments	
Health Concerns	
Plans for Tommorow	
Pain Level	
Happiness Level	
Alertness Level	
Supplies Needed Soon	
Medication Taken	

Notes

Caregiving Notes for						Date		
Toileting Time								
U								
BM								
Waking Up at Night								
Breakfast								
AM Snack								
Lunch								
PM Snack								
Dinner								
Drinks								

Activities

Appointments	
Health Concerns	
Plans for Tommorow	
Pain Level	
Happiness Level	
Alertness Level	
Supplies Needed Soon	
Medication Taken	

Notes

Caregiving Notes for						Date		
Toileting	Time							
	U							
	BM							
Waking Up at Night								
Breakfast								
AM Snack								
Lunch								
PM Snack								
Dinner								
Drinks								

Activities	

Appointments	
Health Concerns	
Plans for Tommorow	
Pain Level	
Happiness Level	
Alertness Level	
Supplies Needed Soon	
Medication Taken	

Notes	

Caregiving Notes for						Date		
Toileting	Time							
	U							
	BM							
Waking Up at Night								
Breakfast								
AM Snack								
Lunch								
PM Snack								
Dinner								
Drinks								

Activities	

Appointments	
Health Concerns	
Plans for Tommorow	
Pain Level	
Happiness Level	
Alertness Level	
Supplies Needed Soon	
Medication Taken	

Notes	

Caregiving Notes for								Date		
Toileting	Time									
	U									
	BM									
Waking Up at Night										
Breakfast										
AM Snack										
Lunch										
PM Snack										
Dinner										
Drinks										

Activities	

Appointments	
Health Concerns	
Plans for Tommorow	
Pain Level	
Happiness Level	
Alertness Level	
Supplies Needed Soon	
Medication Taken	

Notes	

Caregiving Notes for						Date		
Toileting	Time							
	U							
	BM							
Waking Up at Night								
Breakfast								
AM Snack								
Lunch								
PM Snack								
Dinner								
Drinks								

Activities	

Appointments	
Health Concerns	
Plans for Tommorow	
Pain Level	
Happiness Level	
Alertness Level	
Supplies Needed Soon	
Medication Taken	

Notes	

Caregiving Notes for								
Toileting	Time							
	U							
	BM							
Waking Up at Night								
Breakfast								
AM Snack								
Lunch								
PM Snack								
Dinner								
Drinks								

Date

Activities

Appointments	
Health Concerns	
Plans for Tommorow	
Pain Level	
Happiness Level	
Alertness Level	
Supplies Needed Soon	
Medication Taken	

Notes

Caregiving Notes for						Date		
Toileting	Time							
	U							
	BM							
Waking Up at Night								
Breakfast								
AM Snack								
Lunch								
PM Snack								
Dinner								
Drinks								

Activities	

Appointments	
Health Concerns	
Plans for Tommorow	
Pain Level	
Happiness Level	
Alertness Level	
Supplies Needed Soon	
Medication Taken	

Notes	

Caregiving Notes for						Date		
Toileting	Time							
	U							
	BM							
Waking Up at Night								
Breakfast								
AM Snack								
Lunch								
PM Snack								
Dinner								
Drinks								

Activities	

Appointments	
Health Concerns	
Plans for Tommorow	
Pain Level	
Happiness Level	
Alertness Level	
Supplies Needed Soon	
Medication Taken	

Notes	

Caregiving Notes for								
Toileting	Time							
	U							
	BM							
Waking Up at Night								
Breakfast								
AM Snack								
Lunch								
PM Snack								
Dinner								
Drinks								

Date

Activities	

Appointments	
Health Concerns	
Plans for Tommorow	
Pain Level	
Happiness Level	
Alertness Level	
Supplies Needed Soon	
Medication Taken	

Notes	

Caregiving Notes for						Date		
Toileting	Time							
	U							
	BM							
Waking Up at Night								
Breakfast								
AM Snack								
Lunch								
PM Snack								
Dinner								
Drinks								

Activities	

Appointments	
Health Concerns	
Plans for Tommorow	
Pain Level	
Happiness Level	
Alertness Level	
Supplies Needed Soon	
Medication Taken	

Notes	

Caregiving Notes for						Date		
Toileting	Time							
	U							
	BM							
Waking Up at Night								
Breakfast								
AM Snack								
Lunch								
PM Snack								
Dinner								
Drinks								

Activities

Appointments	
Health Concerns	
Plans for Tommorow	
Pain Level	
Happiness Level	
Alertness Level	
Supplies Needed Soon	
Medication Taken	

Notes

Caregiving Notes for						Date		
Toileting	Time							
	U							
	BM							
Waking Up at Night								
Breakfast								
AM Snack								
Lunch								
PM Snack								
Dinner								
Drinks								

Activities	

Appointments	
Health Concerns	
Plans for Tommorow	
Pain Level	
Happiness Level	
Alertness Level	
Supplies Needed Soon	
Medication Taken	

Notes	

Caregiving Notes for								
Toileting	Time							
	U							
	BM							

Date

Waking Up at Night		
Breakfast	
AM Snack	
Lunch	
PM Snack	
Dinner	
Drinks	

Activities

Appointments

Health Concerns

Plans for Tommorow

Pain Level

Happiness Level

Alertness Level

Supplies Needed Soon

Medication Taken

Notes

Caregiving Notes for						Date		
Toileting	Time							
	U							
	BM							
Waking Up at Night								
Breakfast								
AM Snack								
Lunch								
PM Snack								
Dinner								
Drinks								

Activities	

Appointments	
Health Concerns	
Plans for Tommorow	
Pain Level	
Happiness Level	
Alertness Level	
Supplies Needed Soon	
Medication Taken	

Notes	

Caregiving Notes for						Date		
Toileting	Time							
	U							
	BM							
Waking Up at Night								
Breakfast								
AM Snack								
Lunch								
PM Snack								
Dinner								
Drinks								

Activities	

Appointments	
Health Concerns	
Plans for Tommorow	
Pain Level	
Happiness Level	
Alertness Level	
Supplies Needed Soon	
Medication Taken	

Notes	

Caregiving Notes for						Date		
Toileting	Time							
	U							
	BM							
Waking Up at Night								
Breakfast								
AM Snack								
Lunch								
PM Snack								
Dinner								
Drinks								

Activities	

Appointments	
Health Concerns	
Plans for Tommorow	
Pain Level	
Happiness Level	
Alertness Level	
Supplies Needed Soon	
Medication Taken	

Notes	

Caregiving Notes for						Date		
Toileting	Time							
	U							
	BM							
Waking Up at Night								
Breakfast								
AM Snack								
Lunch								
PM Snack								
Dinner								
Drinks								

Activities

Appointments

Health Concerns

Plans for Tommorow

Pain Level

Happiness Level

Alertness Level

Supplies Needed Soon

Medication Taken

Notes

Caregiving Notes for						Date		
Toileting	Time							
	U							
	BM							
Waking Up at Night								
Breakfast								
AM Snack								
Lunch								
PM Snack								
Dinner								
Drinks								

Activities	

Appointments	
Health Concerns	
Plans for Tommorow	
Pain Level	
Happiness Level	
Alertness Level	
Supplies Needed Soon	
Medication Taken	

Notes	

Caregiving Notes for						Date		
Toileting	Time							
	U							
	BM							
Waking Up at Night								
Breakfast								
AM Snack								
Lunch								
PM Snack								
Dinner								
Drinks								

Activities	

Appointments	
Health Concerns	
Plans for Tommorow	
Pain Level	
Happiness Level	
Alertness Level	
Supplies Needed Soon	
Medication Taken	

Notes	

Caregiving Notes for						Date		
Toileting	Time							
	U							
	BM							
Waking Up at Night								
Breakfast								
AM Snack								
Lunch								
PM Snack								
Dinner								
Drinks								

Activities	

Appointments	
Health Concerns	
Plans for Tommorow	
Pain Level	
Happiness Level	
Alertness Level	
Supplies Needed Soon	
Medication Taken	

Notes	

Caregiving Notes for						Date		
Toileting	Time							
	U							
	BM							
Waking Up at Night								
Breakfast								
AM Snack								
Lunch								
PM Snack								
Dinner								
Drinks								

Activities	

Appointments	
Health Concerns	
Plans for Tommorow	
Pain Level	
Happiness Level	
Alertness Level	
Supplies Needed Soon	
Medication Taken	

Notes	

Caregiving Notes for						Date		
Toileting	Time							
	U							
	BM							
Waking Up at Night								
Breakfast								
AM Snack								
Lunch								
PM Snack								
Dinner								
Drinks								

Activities	

Appointments	
Health Concerns	
Plans for Tommorow	
Pain Level	
Happiness Level	
Alertness Level	
Supplies Needed Soon	
Medication Taken	

Notes	

Caregiving Notes for								
	Time							
Toileting	U							
	BM							

Date

Waking Up at Night				

Breakfast	
AM Snack	
Lunch	
PM Snack	
Dinner	
Drinks	

Activities	

Appointments	
Health Concerns	
Plans for Tommorow	
Pain Level	
Happiness Level	
Alertness Level	
Supplies Needed Soon	
Medication Taken	

Notes	

Caregiving Notes for						Date			
Toileting	Time								
	U								
	BM								
Waking Up at Night									
Breakfast									
AM Snack									
Lunch									
PM Snack									
Dinner									
Drinks									

Activities	

Appointments	
Health Concerns	
Plans for Tommorow	
Pain Level	
Happiness Level	
Alertness Level	
Supplies Needed Soon	
Medication Taken	

Notes	

Caregiving Notes for						Date			
Toileting	Time								
	U								
	BM								
Waking Up at Night									
Breakfast									
AM Snack									
Lunch									
PM Snack									
Dinner									
Drinks									

Activities

Appointments	
Health Concerns	
Plans for Tommorow	
Pain Level	
Happiness Level	
Alertness Level	
Supplies Needed Soon	
Medication Taken	

Notes

Caregiving Notes for						Date		
Toileting	Time							
	U							
	BM							
Waking Up at Night								
Breakfast								
AM Snack								
Lunch								
PM Snack								
Dinner								
Drinks								

Activities

Appointments	
Health Concerns	
Plans for Tommorow	
Pain Level	
Happiness Level	
Alertness Level	
Supplies Needed Soon	
Medication Taken	

Notes

Caregiving Notes for						Date		
Toileting	Time							
	U							
	BM							
Waking Up at Night								
Breakfast								
AM Snack								
Lunch								
PM Snack								
Dinner								
Drinks								

Activities	

Appointments	
Health Concerns	
Plans for Tommorow	
Pain Level	
Happiness Level	
Alertness Level	
Supplies Needed Soon	
Medication Taken	

Notes	

Caregiving Notes for						Date		
Toileting	Time							
	U							
	BM							
Waking Up at Night								
Breakfast								
AM Snack								
Lunch								
PM Snack								
Dinner								
Drinks								

Activities

Appointments	
Health Concerns	
Plans for Tommorow	
Pain Level	
Happiness Level	
Alertness Level	
Supplies Needed Soon	
Medication Taken	

Notes

Caregiving Notes for						Date		
Toileting	Time							
	U							
	BM							
Waking Up at Night								
Breakfast								
AM Snack								
Lunch								
PM Snack								
Dinner								
Drinks								

Activities

Appointments	
Health Concerns	
Plans for Tommorow	
Pain Level	
Happiness Level	
Alertness Level	
Supplies Needed Soon	
Medication Taken	

Notes

Caregiving Notes for						Date		
Toileting	Time							
	U							
	BM							
Waking Up at Night								
Breakfast								
AM Snack								
Lunch								
PM Snack								
Dinner								
Drinks								

Activities

Appointments	
Health Concerns	
Plans for Tommorow	
Pain Level	
Happiness Level	
Alertness Level	
Supplies Needed Soon	
Medication Taken	

Notes

Caregiving Notes for						Date		
Toileting	Time							
	U							
	BM							
Waking Up at Night								
Breakfast								
AM Snack								
Lunch								
PM Snack								
Dinner								
Drinks								

Activities

Appointments	
Health Concerns	
Plans for Tommorow	
Pain Level	
Happiness Level	
Alertness Level	
Supplies Needed Soon	
Medication Taken	

Notes

Caregiving Notes for						Date		
Toileting	Time							
	U							
	BM							
Waking Up at Night								
Breakfast								
AM Snack								
Lunch								
PM Snack								
Dinner								
Drinks								

Activities	

Appointments	
Health Concerns	
Plans for Tommorow	
Pain Level	
Happiness Level	
Alertness Level	
Supplies Needed Soon	
Medication Taken	

Notes	

Caregiving Notes for						Date		
Toileting	Time							
	U							
	BM							
Waking Up at Night								
Breakfast								
AM Snack								
Lunch								
PM Snack								
Dinner								
Drinks								

Activities	

Appointments	
Health Concerns	
Plans for Tommorow	
Pain Level	
Happiness Level	
Alertness Level	
Supplies Needed Soon	
Medication Taken	

Notes	

Caregiving Notes for						Date		
Toileting	Time							
	U							
	BM							
Waking Up at Night								
Breakfast								
AM Snack								
Lunch								
PM Snack								
Dinner								
Drinks								

Activities

Appointments

Health Concerns

Plans for Tommorow

Pain Level

Happiness Level

Alertness Level

Supplies Needed Soon

Medication Taken

Notes

Caregiving Notes for								
	Time							
Toileting	U							
	BM							
Waking Up at Night								
Breakfast								
AM Snack								
Lunch								
PM Snack								
Dinner								
Drinks								

Date

Activities	

Appointments	
Health Concerns	
Plans for Tommorow	
Pain Level	
Happiness Level	
Alertness Level	
Supplies Needed Soon	
Medication Taken	

Notes	

Caregiving Notes for						Date		
Toileting	Time							
	U							
	BM							
Waking Up at Night								
Breakfast								
AM Snack								
Lunch								
PM Snack								
Dinner								
Drinks								

Activities	

Appointments	
Health Concerns	
Plans for Tommorow	
Pain Level	
Happiness Level	
Alertness Level	
Supplies Needed Soon	
Medication Taken	

Notes	

Caregiving Notes for						Date		

Toileting	Time							
	U							
	BM							

Waking Up at Night			

Breakfast	
AM Snack	
Lunch	
PM Snack	
Dinner	
Drinks	

Activities	

Appointments	
Health Concerns	
Plans for Tommorow	
Pain Level	
Happiness Level	
Alertness Level	
Supplies Needed Soon	
Medication Taken	

Notes	

Caregiving Notes for								Date	
Toileting	Time								
	U								
	BM								
Waking Up at Night									
Breakfast									
AM Snack									
Lunch									
PM Snack									
Dinner									
Drinks									

Activities

Appointments	
Health Concerns	
Plans for Tommorow	
Pain Level	
Happiness Level	
Alertness Level	
Supplies Needed Soon	
Medication Taken	

Notes

Caregiving Notes for						**Date**		
Toileting	Time							
	U							
	BM							
Waking Up at Night								
Breakfast								
AM Snack								
Lunch								
PM Snack								
Dinner								
Drinks								

Activities

Appointments

Health Concerns

Plans for Tommorow

Pain Level

Happiness Level

Alertness Level

Supplies Needed Soon

Medication Taken

Notes

Caregiving Notes for					Date		
Toileting Time							
U							
BM							

Waking Up at Night			

Breakfast	
AM Snack	
Lunch	
PM Snack	
Dinner	
Drinks	

Activities

Appointments	
Health Concerns	
Plans for Tommorow	
Pain Level	
Happiness Level	
Alertness Level	
Supplies Needed Soon	
Medication Taken	

Notes

Caregiving Notes for						Date		
Toileting	Time							
	U							
	BM							
Waking Up at Night								
Breakfast								
AM Snack								
Lunch								
PM Snack								
Dinner								
Drinks								

Activities	

Appointments	
Health Concerns	
Plans for Tommorow	
Pain Level	
Happiness Level	
Alertness Level	
Supplies Needed Soon	
Medication Taken	

Notes	

Caregiving Notes for						Date		
Toileting	Time							
	U							
	BM							
Waking Up at Night								
Breakfast								
AM Snack								
Lunch								
PM Snack								
Dinner								
Drinks								

Activities	

Appointments	
Health Concerns	
Plans for Tommorow	
Pain Level	
Happiness Level	
Alertness Level	
Supplies Needed Soon	
Medication Taken	

Notes	

Caregiving Notes for						Date		
Toileting Time								
U								
BM								
Waking Up at Night								
Breakfast								
AM Snack								
Lunch								
PM Snack								
Dinner								
Drinks								

Activities

Appointments

Health Concerns

Plans for Tommorow

Pain Level

Happiness Level

Alertness Level

Supplies Needed Soon

Medication Taken

Notes

Caregiving Notes for						Date		
Toileting	Time							
	U							
	BM							
Waking Up at Night								
Breakfast								
AM Snack								
Lunch								
PM Snack								
Dinner								
Drinks								

Activities	

Appointments	
Health Concerns	
Plans for Tommorow	
Pain Level	
Happiness Level	
Alertness Level	
Supplies Needed Soon	
Medication Taken	

Notes	

Caregiving Notes for						Date		
Toileting	Time							
	U							
	BM							
Waking Up at Night								
Breakfast								
AM Snack								
Lunch								
PM Snack								
Dinner								
Drinks								

Activities	

Appointments	
Health Concerns	
Plans for Tommorow	
Pain Level	
Happiness Level	
Alertness Level	
Supplies Needed Soon	
Medication Taken	

Notes	

Caregiving Notes for								
Toileting	Time							
	U							
	BM							

Date

Waking Up at Night			

Breakfast	
AM Snack	
Lunch	
PM Snack	
Dinner	
Drinks	

Activities	

Appointments	
Health Concerns	
Plans for Tommorow	
Pain Level	
Happiness Level	
Alertness Level	
Supplies Needed Soon	
Medication Taken	

Notes	

Made in the USA
Las Vegas, NV
23 October 2024

10317106R00066